W9-ATS-556

June

K. C. KELLEY • BOB OSTROM

Published by The Child's World®
1980 Lookout Drive • Mankato, MN 56003-1705
800-599-READ • www.childsworld.com

Acknowledgments
The Child's World®: Mary Berendes, Publishing Director
The Design Lab: Design
Jody Jensen Shaffer: Editing and Fact-Checking

Photo credits
© 360b/Shutterstock.com: 22 (bottom); Baseball Hall of Fame:
20 (bottom); freya-photographer/Shutterstock.com: 11 (bottom);
Garsya/Shutterstock.com: 6; GeorgiosArt/iStock.com: 22
(top); Georgios Kollidas/Shutterstock.com: 20 (top); Jerry Coli/
Dreamstime.com: 23 (bottom); Joe Robbins: 23 (top); lev radin/
Shutterstockcom: 23 (middle); Louella938 /Shutterstock.com: 13
(top); www.NASA.gov: 19 (bottom); National Media Museum
from UK/Wikimedia Commons: 18; Pavel L Photo and Video/
Shutterstock.com: 11 (top); Richie Lomba/Dreamstime.com :
19 (top); Taeya18/Shutterstock.com: 13 (bottom); Tiplyashina
Evgeniya/Shutterstock.com: 10; Subbotina Anna/Shutterstock.
com: cover, 1, 5; visuelldesign/Shutterstock.com: 12 (top);
Wikimedia Commons: 23 (bottom); ZouZou/Shutterstock.com: 12
(bottom)

ISBN 9781626873681
LCCN 2014930707

Printed in the United States of America
Mankato, MN
July, 2014
PA02214

ABOUT THE AUTHOR

K.C. Kelley has written dozens of books for young readers on
everything from sports to nature to history. He was born in
January, loves April because that's when baseball begins, and
loves to take vacations in August!

ABOUT THE ILLUSTRATOR

Bob Ostrom has been illustrating books for twenty years.
A graduate of the New England School of Art & Design at
Suffolk University, Bob has worked for such companies as
Disney, Nickelodeon, and Cartoon Network. He lives in North
Carolina with his wife and three children.

Contents

WELCOME TO JUNE!

Welcome, summer! Summer begins every June 20 or 21. That means that one of those days is the longest day of the year. People have celebrated this event for thousands of years. It's called the Summer Solstice.

June

FACT BOX

Order: Sixth

Days: 30

With long days and good weather, June is filled with fun. Many people enjoy summer vacations and picnics.

HOW DID JUNE GET ITS NAME?

The ancient Romans called their main female god *Juno*. They named the month of June in her honor.

THREE COOL THINGS ABOUT JUNE

- June joins April and May as months that can also be girls' names!
- In Earth's southern **hemisphere**, June 20 or 21 is the shortest day!
- June is a big month for high school and college **graduation** ceremonies.

Birthstone

Each month has a stone linked to it. People who have birthdays in that month call it their birthstone. For June, it's the pearl. Pearls are actually not stones. They are made inside oysters, which form them over many years.

JUNE AROUND THE WORLD

Here is the name of this month in other languages.

Chinese	Liù yuè
Dutch	Juni
English	June
French	Juin
German	der Juni
Italian	Giugno
Japanese	Rokugatsu
Spanish	Junio
Swahili	Juni

WEDDINGS GALORE!

Many people choose to marry in June. Part of the reason is from ancient Rome. The name for June comes from a Roman god of marriage. June also has the longest days and some of the nicest weather, so wedding celebrations could last a long time.

7

BIG JUNE HOLIDAYS

Summer Solstice

The longest day of the year is often a big party day! In Europe, it's called "Midsummer." People hold big festivals. Such celebrations have been held for centuries. People in ancient Britain gathered on the Solstice to enjoy the long day of sunlight. Some believe that Britain's famous Stonehenge monument was built to catch the sun on this day.

JUNETEENTH

The end of slavery is certainly something to celebrate. President Abraham Lincoln had freed slaves in 1863. But on June 19, 1865, Union soldiers finally arrived in Texas. They again declared slavery at an end in that state. That day became a holiday called Juneteenth in Texas. Soon, the idea spread to other states. Today, people celebrate Juneteenth as a day of freedom. They have barbecues, church services, and speeches.

Flag Day, June 14

On June 14, 1777, Congress approved the look of the United States flag. Today we celebrate the "Stars and Stripes" that stand for our country by flying the flag and wearing red, white, and blue.

Father's Day, Third Sunday

The third Sunday in June is for Dads! Father's Day has been an official holiday since 1972.

Children often honor their dads with cards and presents. Some families have picnics and cookouts.

FUN JUNE DAYS

June has more ways to celebrate than just picnics and cookouts! Here are some of the unusual holidays you can enjoy in June:

June 4

Hug Your Cat Day

June 6

National Yo-Yo Day

FIRST FRIDAY

National Donut Day

June 12

Red Rose Day

June 20

American Eagle Day

June 23

National Pink Day

12

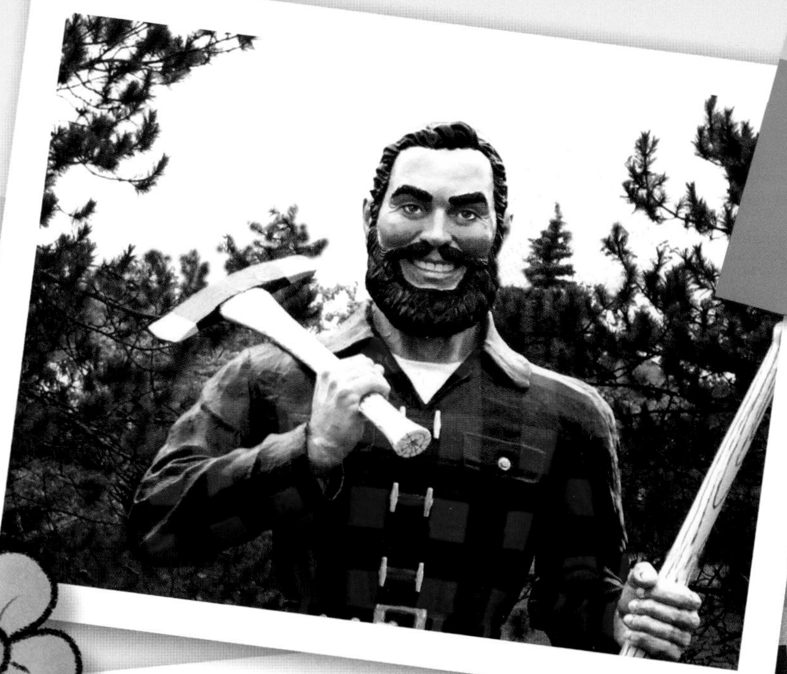

June 28

Paul Bunyan Day

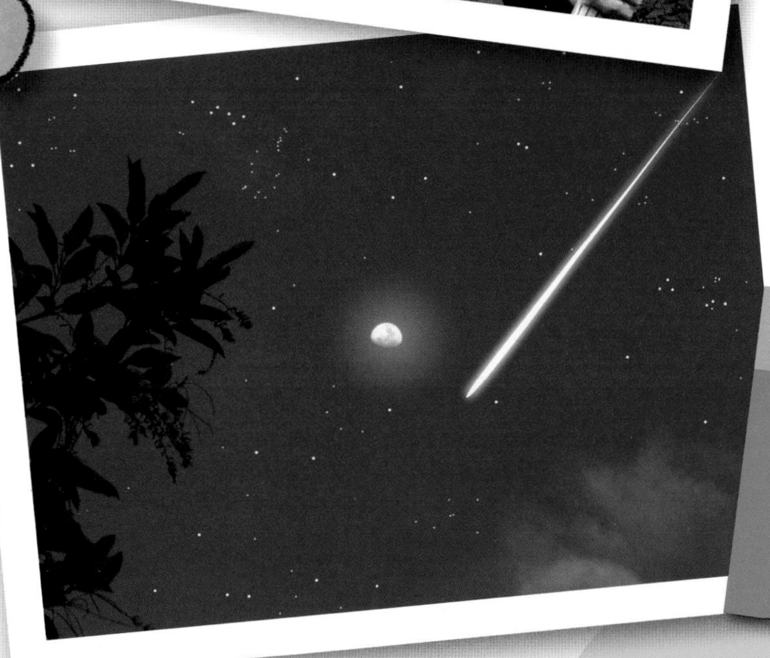

June 30

Meteor Day

JUNE WEEKS AND MONTHS

Holidays don't just mean days...you can celebrate for a week, too! You can also have fun all month long. Find out more about these ways to enjoy June!

JUNE WEEKS

National Fishing and Boating Week: Have you ever tried fishing? It's fun and can teach you about fish and the places they live. During Fishing Week, many areas offer free fishing and lessons on how to fish. Drop a line during Fishing Week!

Duct Tape Days: Duct tape has been used to fix things since the 1940s. Today, people use duct tape for everything! They make wallets, hats, purses, clothes, and even toys! Celebrate this amazing sticky stuff this week by being creative.

JUNE MONTHS

National Candy Month: Right...we know. EVERY month is Candy Month! Well, June is the official month to honor this sweet stuff. Candy is great to eat, but like everything else: Too much of anything is not a good idea. Some estimate that the average American eats 25 pounds of candy a year. That's good news for dentists!

National Accordion Awareness Month: Do you know what an accordion is? This celebration wants to make sure you do! This musical instruments mixes keys like a piano with a squeezebox. The musician wears the accordion on straps. As the air is pushed through, the keys make the music.

National Camping Month: June is a great time to go camping! You can join thousands of folks who pitch a tent, cook outdoors, and make s'mores! Try going camping with several families at once—you can all chip in for the

JUNE AROUND THE WORLD

Countries around the world celebrate in June. Find these countries on the map. Then read about how people there have fun in June!

June 24

Inti Raymi, Peru
This "Festival of the Sun" comes from the ancient Incas. This was the beginning of a new year for those ancient people.

WORLD JUGGLING DAY

On the Saturday nearest June 17, watch out for flying balls, clubs, and more! World Juggling Day spreads the fun of this activity. Jugglers show off their best moves. The best can keep as many as nine balls in the air at once! Have you ever tried to juggle? Here's a tip: start with just one ball. When you're really good with both hands...add one more ball!

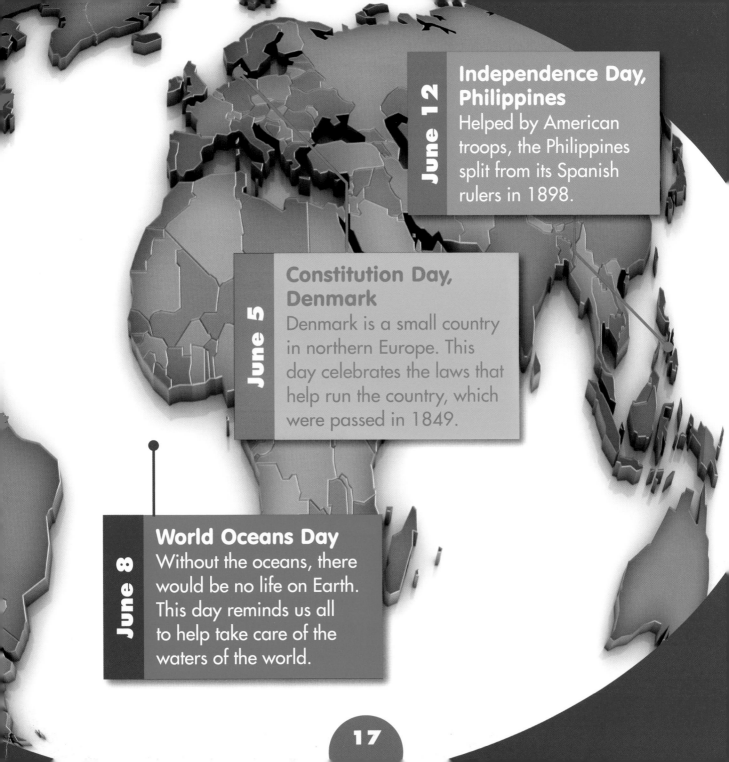

Independence Day, Philippines

June 12

Helped by American troops, the Philippines split from its Spanish rulers in 1898.

Constitution Day, Denmark

June 5

Denmark is a small country in northern Europe. This day celebrates the laws that help run the country, which were passed in 1849.

World Oceans Day

June 8

Without the oceans, there would be no life on Earth. This day reminds us all to help take care of the waters of the world.

JUNE IN HISTORY

June 2, 1953

Elizabeth II became Queen of England.

June 10, 1610

Dutch **colonists** arrive at the island that is now part of New York City. They called it New Amsterdam.

D-DAY

June 6, 1944, is known as D-Day. It was the biggest battle of World War II. German forces controlled France and much of Europe. American and British soldiers landed in France on this day. More than 11,000 aircraft and two million men took part in the attack. They rode across the English Channel in more than 6,000 boats. Thousands were killed or hurt that day, but they fought on. Their bravery helped free Europe from the **Nazis**.

June 12, 1939

The Baseball Hall of Fame opened in Cooperstown, New York.

June 15, 1775

George Washington got a new job—commander of the Continental Army. He led the Army to victory in the American Revolution.

June 18, 1928

Amelia Earhart landed in France. She was the first woman to fly across the Atlantic Ocean.

June 18, 1983

Astronaut Sally Ride became the first American woman in space.

June 18, 1815

British troops beat the French emperor Napoleon at the Battle of Waterloo.

June 19, 1846

What some people call the "first" baseball game was played in New Jersey. The sport had been played before, but this game used rules much like today's game.

NEW STATES!

Six states first joined the United States in June. Do you live in any of these? If you do, then make sure and say, "Happy Birthday!" to your state.

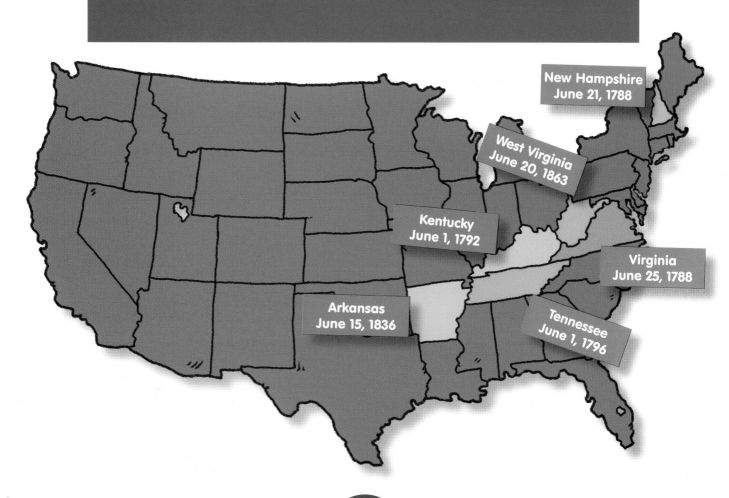

New Hampshire
June 21, 1788

West Virginia
June 20, 1863

Kentucky
June 1, 1792

Virginia
June 25, 1788

Arkansas
June 15, 1836

Tennessee
June 1, 1796

FAMOUS JUNE BIRTHDAYS

June 2

Martha Washington
The wife of George Washington, she was the very first "First Lady" of the United States.

June 6

The Dalai Lama
The Dalai Lama (DAH-lay LAH-ma) leads the faith called Tibetan Buddhism.

June 9

Johnny Depp
This star plays Captain Jack Sparrow in pirate movies.

June 11

Joe Montana

As the San Francisco 49ers quarterback, Montana won four Super Bowls.

June 17

Venus Williams

This amazing tennis star has won 17 Grand Slam finals, fifth most all-time.

June 27

Helen Keller

She could not hear, see, or talk. Yet with the help of teachers, Helen became a world-famous writer and speaker.

June 28

John Elway

This Hall-of-Famer passer led the Broncos to two Super Bowl wins.

GLOSSARY

colonists (KOLL-uh-nists) People who live in newly settled areas.

graduation (grad-yoo-AY-shun) A ceremony for someone who has completed the last year in a school.

hemisphere (HEM-iss-feer) Earth is divided into two halves—the northern hemisphere and the southern hemisphere. Australia is in the southern hemisphere.

Nazis (NAHT-zees) A group that ruled Germany from 1933–1945. They believed certain groups of people, such as Jews and Gypsies, should not be part of the human race.

Summer Solstice (SUM-mur SOHL-stiss) A time when Earth is closest to the sun. It is the longest day of the year in the northern hemisphere.

INDEX